TO:

FROM:

Leesa McGregor

A New Alphabet For Humanity

illustrated by Daniela Sosa

Dear Parents and Teachers,

My name is Leesa McGregor. I have dedicated my life's work to making a difference and inspiring positive change. I have always believed that our thoughts and words have the power to shape our lives.

After having my son, I started to imagine how different the world would be if children were taught words like compassion, empathy and diversity from an early age. From there, an idea was born, to create a New Alphabet for Humanity.

Inside this book, you'll discover a delightful way to empower children to connect with their hearts and become the best version of themselves. To learn the power of positive words that can instill the values and qualities we all desire to live by. To be compassionate, kind and loving to people and the planet.

You can use this book as a talking piece, to create meaningful connections and conversations that bring out the best in your child. The concepts contained in A New Alphabet for Humanity are a great source of inspiration for young children and adults!

My vision for this book is to nurture the heart, imagination and potential of children all around the world.

To parents, and teachers everywhere, thank you for sharing this alphabet with the children in your life.

Together, we can change the world.

Love,
Leesa

To receive a free Printable Alphabet
Poster and Lesson Plan, simply go to
www.AlphabetforHumanity.com

I dedicate this book to all the children of the world.

May you grow to be happy, loving, peaceful and free,
knowing you are never too small to make a difference.

- Leesa McGregor

A is for Abundance

Abundance is knowing there is enough for you and enough for me. The more I give to others, the more I receive.

B is for Bravery

**Bravery is having the courage to try new things.
I am brave when I do something I've never done before.**

C is for Compassion

**Compassion is showing kindness and care for others.
I have compassion when I help someone in need.**

D is for Diversity

**Diversity is accepting people who are different from me.
While we may be different, on the inside we are all the same.**

E is for Empathy

**Empathy is understanding how another person is feeling.
I have empathy when I imagine myself in someone else's shoes.**

F is for Forgiveness

Forgiveness is letting go of hurt feelings when someone upsets me. Forgiveness is holding love in my heart instead.

G is for Gratitude

Gratitude is thinking about all the things that make me smile.
I am grateful when I give thanks for my day and the people I love.

H is for Happiness

**Happiness is feeling cheerful and excited in my body.
I am happy when I follow my heart and make time to play.**

I is for Imagination

Imagination is making a picture in my mind about what I would like to be. When I use my imagination, anything is possible.

J is for Joyful

**Joyful is a warm and happy feeling in my heart.
I am joyful when I have fun doing what I love.**

K is for Kind

**Kind is being caring and helpful to others.
I am kind when I do something nice to brighten someone's day.**

L is for Loving

Loving is treating people with respect and gentle care.
When I love myself, my love for others grows and grows.

M is for Mindful

**Mindful is noticing what is happening inside of me and around me.
I am mindful when I take a moment to pause and breathe.**

N is for Nurturing

**Nurturing is caring for people and our big beautiful world.
I am nurturing when I show my love for the earth.**

O is for Optimistic

**Optimistic is always looking on the bright side of life.
I am optimistic when I expect good things to happen.**

P is for Peaceful

**Peaceful is feeling calm inside and knowing all is well.
Peace in the world begins with peace in my heart.**

Q is for Quality

**Quality is the time I spend with my family doing things together.
Quality is also having good toys that last a long time.**

R is for Respectful

**Respectful is being kind to people and nature.
I am respectful when I help take care of the world around me.**

S is for Sincere

**Sincere is being truthful and honest with others.
I am sincere when I say something that comes from my heart.**

T is for Thankful

**Thankful is appreciating all of the wonderful things in my life.
I am thankful when I enjoy special moments with family and friends.**

U is for Unity

Unity is knowing we are all connected to each other as one big human family. Together we can change the world.

V is for Vibrant

**Vibrant is feeling happy and full of energy in my body.
I am vibrant when I eat healthy food and spend time in nature.**

W is for Wise

Wise is knowing the little things I do every day make a big difference. I am wise when I take time to learn and grow.

X is for Exhale

Exhale is the sound I make when I breathe in and let it out.
When I take a deep breath and exhale, I feel calm and relaxed.

Y is for Yes

**Yes is being open to new ideas and experiences.
When I say yes, I discover the fun of new people and places.**

Z is for Zen

Zen is feeling peaceful and relaxed. I am zen when I live in the present moment, the happiest place to be.

We hope you enjoyed this inspiring and empowering book.

To receive a FREE Printable Alphabet Poster and
Lesson Plan, visit: www.AlphabetforHumanity.com

EMPOWERING QUESTIONS:

Here are some simple ways you can continue the conversation with your child about the words contained in A New Alphabet for Humanity.

Showing Compassion

Compassion helps us to take care of each other and uplift everyone around us. When you show compassion, it makes you feel joyful and it helps other people.

Can you think of a time when you felt compassion for another person?
What are some other ways you can show compassion?
How can you show compassion for yourself?

Examples of Compassion:

- Offering to help an elderly person in your community.
- Caring for a family member when they are sick.
- Listening to a friend when they are feeling sad or upset.

Practicing Gratitude

Gratitude helps you to pay attention to all the wonderful things in your life. When you practice gratitude, it helps to you enjoy life and feel happy inside.

What are you grateful for?
What made you laugh or smile today?
How can you show gratitude to others?

Examples of Gratitude:

- Thinking about how much you love your family.
- Remembering how much fun you had at the playground.
- Thanking a family member for making a delicious meal.
- Thinking about how much you enjoy playing with a special toy.

There is always something to be grateful for.

Being Kind

Every person that is kind makes the world a little brighter.
When you are kind, it makes you feel good and it makes others feel good too.

What are some ways you can show kindness to others?
Can you think of something kind you did for another person?
When did you notice someone being kind to another person?

Examples of Being Kind:

- Giving someone a compliment.
- Sharing your toys with a friend.
- Opening the door for someone.

Being Respectful

Respectful is treating others in a way
that makes them feel cared for and valued.
You are also being respectful when you
do things that help take care of the earth.

Can you think of something you did today that was respectful?
What are three ways you can be respectful toward others?
What are some things you can do to help take care of the earth?

Examples of Being Respectful:

- Saying something courteous and polite.
- Treating other people fairly.
- Planting a tree in the earth.
- Keeping our forests and oceans clean.

For more ideas and inspiration,
PLUS a free Prinatble Alphabet
Poster and Lesson Plan, please visit
www.AlphabetforHumanity.com

Thank you for being part of this movement to empower our children and create a bright future for humanity!

About Leesa McGregor

Leesa McGregor is a passionate mother dedicated to making a difference and inspiring positive change. This is her second children's book: her first was 'Around the World Adventures with Max'. Leesa is also a speaker, changemaker and entrepreneur with 20 years' experience growing purpose-driven businesses. You can find her online at www.leesamcgregor.com.

About Daniela Sosa

Originally from Romania, Daniela now lives in Cambridge, UK with her husband, working as a full-time freelance illustrator and enjoying a wide variety of clients across publishing and advertising. Creating a magical mix of the ordinary and extraordinary, Daniela loves to highlight subtle detail and find beauty in everyday life. You can find her online at www.danielasosa.com